A Beginner's Guide to Internet Marketing

17 Proven Marketing Strategies to
Make Money Online and
Grow Your Online Business

KENNETH LEWIS

Copyright 2015 by Kenneth Lewis - All rights reserved.

This document is geared towards providing exact and reliable information in regards to the topic and issue covered. The publication is sold with the idea that the publisher is not required to render accounting, officially permitted, or otherwise, qualified services. If advice is necessary, legal or professional, a practiced individual in the profession should be ordered.

From a Declaration of Principles which was accepted and approved equally by a Committee of the American Bar Association and a Committee of Publishers and Associations.

In no way is it legal to reproduce, duplicate, or transmit any part of this document in either electronic means or in printed format. Recording of this publication is strictly prohibited and any storage of this document is not allowed unless with written permission from the publisher. All rights reserved.

The information provided herein is stated to be truthful and consistent, in that any liability, in terms of inattention or otherwise, by any usage or abuse of any policies, processes, or directions contained within is the solitary and utter responsibility of the recipient reader. Under no circumstances will any legal responsibility or blame be held against the publisher for any reparation, damages, or monetary loss due to the information herein, either directly or indirectly.

Respective authors own all copyrights not held by the publisher.

The information herein is offered for informational purposes solely, and is universal as so. The presentation of the information is without contract or any type of guarantee assurance.

The trademarks that are used are without any consent, and the publication of the trademark is without permission or backing by the trademark owner. All trademarks and brands within this book are for clarifying purposes only and are the owned by the owners themselves, not affiliated with this document.

ISBN: 1519586191
ISBN-13: 978-1519586193

DEDICATED TO
THE READER

May you achieve success in all your business
and entrepreneurial endeavors.

TABLE OF CONTENTS

i	Introduction	1
1	Important Considerations and General Advice on Internet Marketing	7
2	Introductory Concepts	15
3	Types of Online Marketing	25
4	Customer Connection	35
5	Additional Targeting and Testing Methods	41
ii	Conclusion	47
iii	Bonus Excerpt: *Facebook Marketing: How to Use Facebook for Effective Internet Marketing and Social Media Success*	57
iv	Other Works by Kenneth Lewis	67
v	About the Author	71

INTRODUCTION

The World Wide Web might just be the most important invention of the twentieth century. At the very least it is already, inarguably, going to be one of the dominant factors of the twenties. The internet has already penetrates every aspect of our lives – our communication with other people, the way we work, the way we find information, entertain ourselves, organize our lives and most relevantly of all, how we shop.

If you have a business, product or service that you are trying to sell, then the vast array of opportunities that the internet presents is simply far too good to pass up. In this day and age, it is simply essential that if you want to sell something, you are using the internet to help you do it.

The only reason that many businesses are yet to take up the rewarding challenge of using the internet for their own profitable intents is that they are simply not aware of the myriad of different techniques that can be used, or lack the know-how to get their internet marketing campaign off the ground. Most people think the only way the internet can help their business is through a business website, but that is only the beginning – there is so much more out there that you can be doing.

Fortunately, this helpful guide exists to give you and your business the run-down on 17 tried and tested internet marketing strategies. *Do you know what search engine optimization is and how to use it for your own ends? Do you blog, guest blog, or exploit affiliate marketing techniques? Are you using loyalty schemes and user generated content to make your business better?*

If the answer to these questions is no or "I don't know what those words mean" then you have come to the right place! Even if you think you know your internet marketing jargon, this book will still serve as a fast-paced refresher course and a great reference guide.

Congratulations on taking the initiative to improve you online marketing strategy. I trust you will enjoy and benefit from reading.

1

IMPORTANT CONSIDERATIONS AND GENERAL ADVICE ON INTERNET MARKETING

Before we discuss the 17 proven strategies and techniques provided to improve your online marketing campaign provided in this book, it is important to first take a moment to reflect carefully and consider a few wise words of caution.

Firstly, if something seems to be too good to be true, it probably is. This is great advice for anything involving your money, but it is especially true in the realm of online marketing. Major companies like Amazon, Ebay and Google have already nearly secured the lion's share, if not an outright control, on most internet marketing strategies – if you use an internet marketing technique, chances are they are either using this technique better than you or getting a slice of the pie, in one way or another.

Owing to this, many internet gurus are now trying to advocate new, exciting internet marketing techniques, for a price. However, if you haven't heard of their technique before or you can't find further information about it elsewhere, it is likely useless or an outright scam.

Similarly, always think twice about buying lessons on online marketing. One key online marketing principle is realizing that your knowledge and skills are assets that can be taught and thus can earn you money. However, a good student doesn't necessarily make a good teacher, and many internet gurus are trying to use their marketing and supposed authority to promote their vacuous content for a cheap money grab. If you do invest in online marketing courses always research whatever you are buying. If you can't find reliable sources to support it, then it might not be worth your time or your money.

Secondly, if you are to be successful marketing online you will need to have a unique idea. Generally, this is a strong principle to maintain in any business, however even mundane and widespread business ideas can be successful in the real world if they have other factors working for them such as geographical location or a stranglehold on local markets. However, for internet markets and businesses these situational factors are far less important and cannot be relied upon to get you your deserved profit, so the need for uniqueness is greater.

If the product you are selling is not entirely developed and conceptualized by you or your company then it stands a chance that someone else is flogging online somewhere.

Furthermore, this competition will have the advantage

of being around earlier, giving them an established reputation, an existing clientele and more experience than you have. Particularly if you are trying to compete with the mega multi-million brands for a slice of their market share, you simply won't get anywhere if you are thinking that you will do exactly the same thing.

Therefore, you must sincerely and honestly ask yourself: *what makes your product or your company worth buying? What makes your product different, or better?* You will need to have a genuine angle if you are to succeed. Perhaps your products are of better quality or at cheaper price, perhaps you can tailor to the individual or mass market better than your peers, or perhaps your products are made using local materials (or are more environmentally friendly). There are potentially hundreds, if not thousands distinctive approaches to any product, so if it's already out there, try to make your product different (as well as better!).

On a similar vein, the third point that needs to be made here is brand identity. When people are looking at your website or your product, they themselves need to know what you angle is. Even if you have a special product or a great advantage on other market retailers, it will be difficult to succeed if you unable to effectively communicate this.

For example, many food supermarkets offer the entire range of similar products with only slightly variations. However, like you, these supermarkets will have an angle on their competition – they will aim to be cheaper, or produce food of better quality or more morally responsible, etc. However, your major brands will carefully and tactfully promote a consistent image so people know this. When advertising, they may aggressively point out what food they are selling cheaper than their peers and the exact savings you can make. They may romanticize the luxury and elegance of their food. Therefore, people who are looking for cheapness or quality know where to go.

Ultimately, before you consider launching an internet marketing campaign you must approach anything you read or learn about with healthy skepticism. You should also know your brand identity, your product and its angle on the market well in advance.

2

INTRODUCTORY CONCEPTS

STRATEGIES #1 - 6

1 – Website Marketing

Website marketing is the most obvious and straightforward aspect of internet marketing – having a website so that individuals can find you. This website should contain contact details: your company email and phone numbers, the physical location of your company and your opening hours (if your company works in such a way that this is relevant). However, above and beyond your contact details, it is also one of the easiest ways to promote your products. You can demonstrate examples of your work and show your products, you can list good reviews of your services and experiences of your products. A website also allows you to create special offers – discount sales or bundle offers etc., which you may not have space to advertise through other mediums.

In addition to this, a website also serves as a platform to promote loyalty and user-generated content, two powerful interne marketing techniques mentioned later in this guide.

When making a website, it is especially important that your website is crystal clear and very responsive. If you are not familiar with website design and building then using a website builder such as Wix, or investing in a professional, individualized help is well worth the price.

#2 – Search Engine Optimization

Whenever someone wants to find anything on the internet, chances are that person is going to use an internet search engine like Google or Bing. Getting your website or product to be one of the first few displayed is the purpose of search engine optimization. Generally, people are not willing to scroll through dozens of search page results – they will settle on the best thing they can find in the first page, or maybe the second. If your website or product is on the fifth page of websites like Google then these searchers are not likely to find you.

There are a couple of tricks to improve your search engine optimization. One of the most important of these is to learn and manipulate key words in your product's descriptions and titles. When people use search engines they enter certain words more often than others, and psychologically place more value on certain phrases than others. Making sure your product's descriptions and your website content have a healthy frequency of these keywords will help them rank higher on search engines. Simply researching your competition and using services like *Google Keywords* is a great way to discover these key words for yourself.

3 – Traffic Generation

Traffic generation refers to a cluster of techniques that aims to improve the amount of people viewing whatever product, business or service you are promoting. Naturally, without anyone viewing your products or services, the chances that people will be spending money and making you profits is zero. Furthermore, high traffic levels themselves can be monetized through having other websites and products advertised on your website or blog through methods such as pay-per-click schemes.

The formerly mentioned technique, search engine optimization, is one popular way to increase traffic generation, but there are vast amounts of alternative methods you can use. This list includes, but is not limited to, blogging, guest blogging, social media campaigns, user recommendations and reviews and website advertising.

The most important point to remember here is that you *will* need internet traffic – your product is useless if no-one knows about it. Additionally, it is important to start to generate traffic early on, whilst your website, blog or product is still fresh.

4 – Social Media Marketing

Millions of people check their feeds on multiple social networks every day. The potential to generate traffic and sell your products and services to these people is huge. There are just so many websites with vast user bases - Google, Facebook, Instagram, Twitter, Pinterest, Youtube – the list goes on.

The first step to take here is to create various social media accounts for your business. Twitter is a fantastic place to keep your clientele and potential customers updated with short, snappy info-bites, whilst Facebook can give your customer base a more intimate experience with your business, allowing you to post pictures, videos and be more interactive. Pinterest and Instagram are particularly great resources if you have a lot of photos and videos to share – their minimalistic, aesthetically pleasing layout is easy to browse through and rewarding to follow.

However, you must keep these accounts active and interesting! Do not sign up for several accounts if you cannot provide new content on a regular and consistent basis. The more activity you post, the more your clientele will be reminded of your existence and share it with the world, increasing your social media presence. Conversely, as a word of warning, do not spam your followers either – bad, boring content is worse than no content at all.

Additionally, if you have a website or application, make an effort to embed social media activity into it. Add buttons inviting users to share their experiences with your products.

5 – Blogging

A blog is a type of website you use to tell people about your experience, knowledge and ideas as if you were writing a diary entry. Blogs are usually highly simplified and very easy to manage. There are several platforms, such as WordPress.com or Tumblr.com, that can host your blog and provide you with easy to use layout and control tools.

However, what you are probably more interested in is how blogging can help your internet marketing efforts and increase your profits. Essentially blogs provide several services; they can generate traffic towards your main website or social media accounts, they can be used as a customer service and interactive tool which can lead to more online purchases of your products (as they are in effect advertisement). Additionally, blogs themselves can be used to generate income through advertisements and pay per click schemes on any traffic associated with the blog. Ultimately, if you are interested in using internet marketing for your business, you will probably want to make a blog.

Blogs should be written in an informal, easy to read and engaging tone of voice and should be full of great content, updated regularly and written in your own unique, but entertaining voice.

6 – Guest Blogging

If you find yourself lacking the time to write your own blog, or conversely have more time to devote to your internet marketing campaign, then guest blogging might be the next move you need to make. Guest blogging is exactly like blogging with the exception that instead of running and managing your own blog, you find a blogger who will allow you to post an entry on their blog. If you can find several bloggers to guest blog for, you can increase your online presence without having to cultivate, grow and maintain your own blog into relevance.

Furthermore, this relationship between the guest blogger and the blog owner is mutually beneficial; for the blog owner, the guest blogger can add a bit of spice to any blog providing a different writing style as well as authority and perspective on any given topic. Similarly, the guest blogger gets the benefits of linking their own blog and social media to the guest post they make, thus improving their search engine optimization and rearing more internet traffic for their own projects.

To start guest blogging, simply research what popular and successful bloggers are doing within your particular market niche or sector. Use the keyword 'guest post' to see where other individuals have successfully guest posted to blogs. Larger blogs, which are run by multiple people, will have ways for visitors to submit their guest blogs. But be aware of the conditions associated with each blog – not every guest post blog you write will be promised to be submitted!

3

TYPES OF ONLINE MARKETING

STRATEGIES #7 - 13

7 – Affiliate Marketing

Affiliate marketing is a method of generating income by helping to refer people to products which they buy online. By providing a helping hand between the consumer looking for the product and the business selling it, you are rewarded a share of the profit by the business – a commission on each product sold.

If you attempt to get a slice of the affiliate marketing pie there are a couple of things to remember. Essentially your role in the relationship between the consumer and the business is that of an advertiser – you are not directly selling anything, but rather, you are informing and convincing people that they want to buy a particular profit. Owing to this, anything you write to increase the sales of a particular product should be more than just telling people to buy it – you want to have an angle on *why* people should buy it. This doesn't have to be anything complex. You can use your perceived authority on your market sector to recommend the best products that you use, or simply advertised products associated with your business which people will want to buy but which is sold by a different business through your website, blog, etc

To start affiliate marketing you can use websites that exist to help network products being sold online to potential affiliate marketers such as paydot.com.

8 – Email Marketing

Email marketing is exactly what it sounds like – using emails to promote your business and products. There are a couple of things to be mindful of here; whenever you email someone information about your business or products, it is best if you have somehow gained the recipients permission to do so. The best way to do this is to have an email subscription service on your blogs or social media accounts, through which people can voluntarily enter their emails to receive updates. This can help provide you with a list of recipients to message about whatever products or offers you are promoting at any given time.

Similarly, you must be honest and consistent about the volume of emails you send your willing recipients. If your email subscriber services claim that you are going to be sending monthly or weekly emails, than it is essential that you stick to that promise and do not start spamming your potential clients with more emails than this – doing so would be a great way to get your emails blocked and lose customers!

#9 – Article Marketing

Article marketing is a type of marketing where you provide helpful articles to people who are encountering some sort of difficulty. These articles are generally offered for free – they are not sold and do not generate any income on their own. However, what these articles can do for you is provide more reasons for people to become acquainted with your brand and can add more links to your main website and social media for search engine optimization. Article marketing creates the impression that you and your business have legitimate authority and knowledge on the subject matter.

Naturally, any article you write will need to be associated with your niche and business sector. Do not write self help articles, for example, if you are selling custom made baked goods! A more reasonable type of article, if you were a baker, might be 'How to make the best scones' or 'Reasons why your cakes are not rising' (and so on).

Promote your articles through your blog, guest blogging, your social media and other websites where which will accept your content.

10 – Display Advertising

Display marketing is perhaps what most people would

traditionally associate with internet marketing – having advertisements that are displayed to the side or bottom of a webpage's and internet videos, the content of which is significant to your business somehow, through which people can be redirected towards your website, products and social media.

There are two important parts about display advertising. The first is to create a well designed ad through clever use of pictures, font and colour. Think about your brand identity, what you're trying to promote and what will catch the eye of internet goers.

The second important component about display advertising is getting your adverts to the right consumers. Advertising anywhere might give you the appearance of more online presence, but it is unlikely to make you money as your adverts will likely be ignored. However, getting people to pay attention to your adverts means that you will need to find the websites and videos your potential consumers are using and then advertise there.

Fortunately, there exist multiple services which can do most of the work for you, such as Google Display Network.

11 – Mobile Advertising

Not everyone has the time to be browsing the

internet via a computer these days. Not only are people separated from their desktop or laptop during periods of work or recreational activity, but it is becoming more and more popular to browse the internet through smart phones. Owing to this, it is starting to become more and more important to use mobile advertising – the tailoring advertisements to mobile phone usage. People may not always use their computer, but you'll rarely find anybody who goes out and about without their mobile.

If you create a website that you want to advertise through a mobile, it is important to remember the website needs to be mobile friendly. The formatting on many websites will go awry when viewed through the smaller screen of a mobile.

You can get started with mobile advertising through liaison with several internet and social media companies such [Twitter Business](#) or [Google Mobile Ads](#).

12 – Native Advertising

Native advertising is a particularly clever and newer form of advertising. Usually when you are designing an advert, for whatever purpose, your primary goal is to stand out from the crowd and be different, eye-catching and unique. Native advertising is exactly the opposite; it is a type of advertising for your business or product which uses the same format and design as the website, application or service which it is being advertised on. To clarify, this means that if you advertise on a particular website, the way in which your advert is formatted, stylized and the style of its writing matches the formatting, stylization and writing style of the hosting webpage.

There are a couple of advantages to this method. Firstly, internet goers are becoming better at filtering advertisements out of their mind when they are looking at a particular webpage and focusing on why they are at that webpage to begin with. By advertising in a 'native' way, internet goers may not even realize what they are looking at is actually an advert. Native advertising can camouflage itself right into website. Furthermore, this makes the website owners happier – their website appears less advert heavy and their branding is less diluted.

13 – Native Language Marketing

The internet offers the opportunity for users from anywhere around the globe to visit your website, blog and social media accounts. Although consumer habits vary wildly from culture to culture and country to country, your product and business could have multinational appeal and could be using foreign consumers to generate profits.

Naturally, however, all these people will not be speaking the same language and any potential customer who visits your website will not spend a dime if they do not understand what is being said or offered no matter how great your product or website is. Additionally, if your website can be viewed in multiple languages but your competitors cannot, this is one easy way to gain an advantage over your competitors. Conversely, if your competition *is* offering multi-language websites while yours isn't, it can also be a reason why you are losing out.

Owing to this, it can be a great idea to invest in making your website readable in multiple languages. You can embed **Google Translate** in your website as a budget option; however the accuracy of this translation service is dubious. Alternatively, you can use language freelancers or website builders that help multi-language implementation, like **Wix**.

4

CUSTOMER CONNECTION

STRATEGIES #14 - 15

#14 – User Generated Content

User generated content refers to any content created by your customers or loyal followers. User generated content could be a review on a service or product that they have bought, activity through an online forum associated with your business or products, or though posting photos or videos. It could simply be social conversation through comments and posts through your social media accounts, website or blog.

User generated content is great for a multitude of reasons. In particular, if there are a number of positive reviews associated with your product or if there are a bunch of people talking about your service, people will be more likely to buy it. Similarly, user generated content is a great advertisement tool. If your users post videos or blogs of them using your product or service in a positive way, more people will be drawn to try it. Furthermore, clever or captivating user-generated content can be repurposed or re-spun in your own advertising efforts – perhaps your users can inadvertently think of great ways to further demonstrate the benefits of your product.

To make the most of user-generated content, invite people to share their photos and experiences on your website, blog and social media. Furthermore, try to search online on large social websites like Facebook, Twitter and Reddit. If you find something funny or interesting, you can draw attention to it with your own social media with an informal reference to the original source, of course.

#15 – Loyalty

Loyalty schemes are any kind of scheme that reward people for sticking with your brand as opposed to another brand. You might offer discounts for repeat purchases or repeat customers, offer a subscription service where customers get special benefits, or provide incentives for people to refer friends or colleagues to your business. You may maintain strong customer support and responsiveness to your customers – strengthening their faith in your service.

Do the math and determine what rewards you can start to give out for loyalty from your customers. If you are unsure how to proceed, often a straightforward point-based system works well. Give people points on each purchase which, given a certain number of points, translates into a particular reward (e.g a free product or a discount, etc.). Offering an initial free advantage is also a great method to get people to begin buying from your brand which can lead to consistent purchases through more long-term loyalty schemes.

5

ADDITIONAL TARGETING AND TESTING METHODS

STRATEGIES #16 - 17

16 – Advertisement Re-targeting

The overwhelming vast majority of internet shoppers do not purchase anything when they initially visit an online seller. They may be simply researching products they are interested in, shopping around for a better deal or found themselves on a seller's webpage by chance.

Advertisement retargeting is an internet marketing technique that works on trying to bring these purchase shy internet shoppers back to the initial internet retailer. This technique works by placing cookies (a type of internet marker, for the uninformed) which tracks what websites these internet shoppers have been to and then places adverts for the internet retailer on the websites that these individual visit. The sustained advertising keeps your brand image in these shoppers' minds and can be highly effective at seeing greater return rates to your website.

You can try advertisement retargeting with services like Adroll.

17 – A/B Testing

As previously mentioned, most internet marketing campaigns for a business or product will prominently feature a website as a platform for promotion, if not an outright e-commerce tool. Yet no matter how ingenious your website design or how much effort you have laboriously poured into your website, there are still likely to be faults and improvements you could employ to make your customer experience better, increase user retention and maximize your profits.

A/B testing is a method that businesses and website builders use to improve their user experiences. Simply put, it is a method where users compare two versions of a similar web page to see which one produces the best experience. A/B testing is inherently scientific in nature. The reputable agencies which undertake A/B testing on your behalf will provide controlled, randomized trials to give you quantitative data which are as close to facts as you will ever receive. If you have doubts about whether your website is working efficiently then consulting A/B testing company, such as **Optimizely** might be the right technique for you.

CONCLUSION

At first the world of internet marketing may seem to be insignificant – what more is there to internet marketing than running a website or a blog? Yet conversely, for the more educated internet goers, the chaotic and lightning paced realm of internet marketing can feel overwhelming vast and beyond the capabilities of small and medium sized businesses.

However, after having read this guide, you should now be confident, informed and well acquainted in the ways in which you can make the internet your best ally in your marketing campaign.

We explored the various types of content you can produce and market – a website, a blog, guest blogging and article marketing. You should be comfortable and familiar with the range of advertising methods to target your potential customers, draw them towards your business and products and then manage to keep them there through methods such as display advertising, mobile advertising, email marketing, loyalty schemes and user-generated content.

We identified the ways to maximize your online

presence and traffic generation, to get everybody and their mother visiting your business website, via techniques such as search engine optimization and clever and witty social media usage.

Ultimately, by having read this book you are now in a great position to make your business conquer the newest and most uncharted frontier of the business world – the internet.

The next step is to go out into the world and launch your internet marketing campaign! I wish you the best of luck – may you achieve success in taking your business to the next level.

SHARE YOUR EXPERIENCE

Finally, if you enjoyed or benefited from this book, then I would like to ask you for a favor:

Would you be kind enough to leave a review for this book on Amazon?

It would be greatly appreciated!

You can visit Amazon.com and search 'Internet Marketing Kenneth Lewis' to be brought to the book's page in which you can leave your feedback.

Thank you, and best of luck on all you online marketing pursuits.

BONUS EXCERPT

FACEBOOK MARKETING:
How to Use Facebook for Effective Internet Marketing and Social Media Success

Introduction

Facebook is a colossal entity with almost 1 billion daily users interacting with each other and checking their newsfeed for updates about the world. With so many people choosing to access Facebook every day, it is no wonder that it has become one of the greatest marketing assets of this decade.

Facebook actively encourages advertisement efforts on their website and other business relations, providing an abundance of tools and systems for both small and large businesses. However, trying to learn how to market through Facebook poses a steep learning curve. Although a few tips and tricks from tried and tested internet marketing guides are applicable, Facebook needs to be tackled as its own creature, with its own rules.

You need to thoroughly understand how Facebook works on a very fundamental level. This includes topics such as how Facebook determines what content is presented through the newsfeed and the underlying concept of the 'reach' and of organic content.

Your knowledge must also extend to the labyrinthine system of paid advertising and marketing. You need to appreciate the different between a boosted post, a paid advertisement and all the different decisions you should have to make, should you want to employ either. It is also critical to know how the auction and bidding systems work; the underlying mechanism which determines the cost and charges associated with advertising on Facebook.

This, however, doesn't even cover the atoms at the tip of the iceberg. You also need to be intimate with the different Facebook business objective goals and the different audiences you can target via all the options Facebook provides. There are the various pricing schemes you can chose, say as pay-per-click, pay-per-impression and optimized pay-per-click that you cannot market without. Additionally, you need to understand the three-part campaign structure of Facebook advertising and the tools offered to manage advertising, such as the power editor.

With these fundamentals covered in the initial chapter, you can then begin to stretch your marketing muscles with Facebook Insights, which presents an entire world of marketing information for you to analyze. If you want to know how many more people liked your content in the past 24 hours, or what your potential reach could be, Facebook Insights is going to be your best friend. Even if you remain mere associates, you need to appreciate Facebook Insights for what the feedback and power it offers you to refine and improve your marketing efforts.

With Facebook Insights now firmly understood, you can start to really bring your marketing tactics to the next level with advanced internet marketing strategies. If you are naïve about dark posting or if you think pixels are just to do with your screen resolution, that the strategies within this book will give you an enlightening wake-up call. Learn how to target niche audiences, improve conversions, create custom audiences and re-target missed buyers through Facebook with the sophisticated and complex opportunities Facebook presents.

With your marketing expertise now reaching intimidating levels of expertise, you will then be presented with all the various resources that you can utilize to give yourself the Facebook marketing edge. Find out where you can access Facebook's free 34 part marketing e-learning course, or where you should be waiting to hear the latest Facebook news and updates.

With your Facebook mastery established, you must be prudent to stay on top of the game by keeping up to date with all the changes and updates Facebook is developing for release in the near future. Facebook puts light itself to shame with just how fast it rushes ahead.

If you simply sit on the knowledge of established techniques without taking the initiative to keep your knowledge fresh, then you will soon find yourself a Facebook novice once more. Learn about highly anticipated changes, such as Facebook Reactions, Facebook Immersive ads and Facebook Connectivity - changes that may shake the foundations of the current Facebook marketing platform we know today.

Chapter 1: Facebook Organic Reach

Originally, all content a user posted on Facebook would be seen by their followers on their news feeds. However, as Facebook became more popular and the average user subscribed to more users, Facebook implemented a system to filter and restrict the amount of content users see. Now, only a portion of content gets seen by followers, which prevents users from feeling overwhelmed as well as protect them viewing from diluted, poor content – or rather content that they simply will not be interested in. This system is called 'Facebook Reach' and refers to how far and how much penetration (i.e reach) your Facebook content achieves.

Facebook reach deals with 'organic' content. Organic refers to content that is naturally filtered through search engine and social media engines. This organic content is then ranked and filtered according to its quality, and thus generates a certain amount of exposure or traffic based on the ranking it receives.

Although most marketers will also employ Facebook Boost and Facebook Paid Advertising, Facebook Reach is where every internet marketer will want to start. If you learn to play the game and abide by the rules, you can still ensure a high amount of your organic content reaches your desired audience. Furthermore, Facebook Reach is free and is a great way for internet marketers to test the shallow waters before they dive in to the deep end.

Facebook Reach uses an algorithm to filter content and decide whether that content is worth your follower's time. The original algorithm, called 'Edgerank' uses three factors (affinity, edge weight and time decay).

Affinity, Weight and Time Decay

Affinity refers to how well two users are known to each other, and how interconnected their lives are. If two users frequently interact across Facebook, frequently tag each other or belong to many of the same groups and share many of the same friends, than these users will have high affinity. Affinity takes into account clicking on user content, liking, commenting, tagging, sharing and friend-ing as measures of connectedness.

It is important to note that affinity is asymmetrical; user A can have a high affinity towards user B without user B having high affinity towards user A.

Additionally, each action you perform on Facebook has a different 'edge weight'. Simply put, certain actions are considered more important and more telling than others. It is easy and non-committal to like or share content. Commenting however, implies a closer relationship between two users. At the very least, it signals more effort. Owing to this, commenting has a higher edge weight than liking and will be more influential in Facebook Edgerank.

To read the rest of 'Facebook Marketing', you can visit Amazon.com and search under 'Kenneth Lewis' to browse the book editions available.

OTHER WORKS BY KENNETH LEWIS

SEO 2016: A Complete Guide to Search Engine Optimization

Facebook Marketing: The 25 Best Strategies on Using Facebook for Advertising, Business and Making Money Online

Passive Income: Make Money Online and Achieve Financial Freedom – How to Make $500 - $12K with Only $50

Social Media Domination: Social Media Marketing Strategies with Facebook, Twitter, YouTube, Instagram and LinkedIn

Procrastination: 7 Simple Strategies to Overcome Procrastination, Increase Productivity and Develop Time Management Strategies for Life

Interview and Get Any Job You Want: Employment Techniques and How to Answer Toughest Interview Questions

All books are available in e-book format, and many are also available in audiobook and paperback format as well. Simply search Amazon.com for details.

ABOUT THE AUTHOR

For over thirty years Kenneth has been active in the marketing and business force, working for various companies as well as pursuing his own independent projects. He has most recently began publishing introductory books on internet marketing and other various aspects of social media as a way to share his passion and interests with those who are new to these domains.

His books aim to be practical, easy to understand and follow. His books also serve as reference guides to those who are already somewhat familiar with the online marketing sector.

In his spare time, Kenneth enjoys golfing, fishing, and spending time with his family at their lake house. Kenneth is also an avid cook and enjoys experimenting with different recipes.

www.ingramcontent.com/pod-product-compliance
Lightning Source LLC
Chambersburg PA
CBHW021017180526
45163CB00005B/1987